Pauline Ashworth

OK José

Or how José saved the day

AF204386

Ernst Klett Verlag
Stuttgart · Leipzig

Als Ergänzung zu dieser Lektüre bieten wir **Downloadmaterialien** für Lehrkräfte für den Unterrichtseinsatz bzw. für die Unterrichtsvorbereitung an. Bitte geben Sie unter **www.klett.de** diesen Online-Link in das Suchfeld ein:

547082-0001

1. Auflage $\quad$ 1 $\quad$ 8 $\quad$ 7 $\quad$ 6 $\quad$ | $\quad$ 2018 $\quad$ 17

Alle Drucke dieser Auflage sind unverändert und können im Unterricht nebeneinander verwendet werden. Die letzten Zahlen bezeichnen jeweils die Auflage und das Jahr des Druckes.

Das Werk und seine Teile sind urheberrechtlich geschützt. Jede Nutzung in anderen als den gesetzlich zugelassenen Fällen bedarf der vorherigen schriftlichen Einwilligung des Verlages. Hinweis zu § 52 a UrhG: Weder das Werk noch seine Teile dürfen ohne eine solche Einwilligung eingescannt und in ein Netzwerk eingestellt werden. Dies gilt auch für Intranets von Schulen und sonstigen Bildungseinrichtungen.
Fotomechanische Wiedergabe nur mit Genehmigung des Verlages.

© Ernst Klett Verlag GmbH, Stuttgart 2008. Alle Rechte vorbehalten.
www.klett.de

Illustrationen: Steffen Wolff, Düsseldorf.
Druck: AZ Druck und Datentechnik, Kempten.
Printed in Germany.
ISBN 978-3-12-547082-8

Contents

Before you read the story

1. *Look at the cover picture. Say what is happening in the picture. How do you think the characters feel here?*

2. *Look at the title of the story. What do you think "save the day" means?*

3. *Look at the lines from the story below and at your answers for questions 1 and 2 again. What do you think the story is about?*

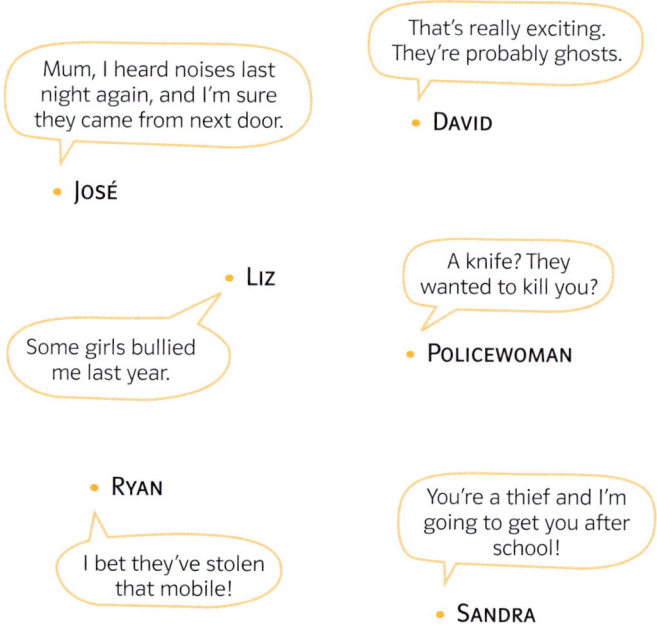

That's really exciting. They're probably ghosts.

• DAVID

Mum, I heard noises last night again, and I'm sure they came from next door.

• JOSÉ

• LIZ

Some girls bullied me last year.

A knife? They wanted to kill you?

• POLICEWOMAN

• RYAN

I bet they've stolen that mobile!

You're a thief and I'm going to get you after school!

• SANDRA

---

bullied ['bʊlid] tyrannisiert, gemobbt • **bet** [bet] wetten, dass • **to get you** [get] *hier:* jemanden kriegen

The house next door

"What's that?"

I've just heard a bang and another strange noise – I don't know what – and I'm sure it came from the house next door. Of course my dog, William, is sleeping and didn't hear anything. He's not really a great help sometimes. He should sleep downstairs in the living room, but he always comes upstairs when everybody is in bed.

• • •

"Mum, I heard noises last night again, and I'm sure they came from next door," I say to my mum at breakfast the next morning.

"Oh, José. But you know that the house next door is empty. Mrs Ross is in hospital, and they don't know when she's going to come out. And you don't believe in ghosts, do you?"

"No, of course I don't," I say, "but maybe we should call the police."

"The police don't have time. They can't come out every time someone hears a bang at night."

"You don't believe me, do you?" I say and I'm angry now. I've heard these noises a few times already and my mum knows that.

"José, of course I believe you, but sometimes it's difficult to know where a noise is coming from. At night everything sounds strange and things often make noises in old houses."

We've just moved house to London because my mother has got a new job here. We've been here a week and I've heard noises on three different nights. I'm sure they're not just bangs. I think someone – or something – is in there and they shouldn't be.

4 of course [əv kɔːs] natürlich • 4 William [ˈwɪljəm] • 11 José [həʊˈzeɪ] • 12 hospital [ˈhɒspɪtl] Krankenhaus • 13 to come out [kʌmˈaʊt] entlassen werden • 17 to come out [kʌmˈaʊt] herkommen • 26 to move house [muːv] umziehen

5

I walk into the garden and look at the house next door. The curtains are closed, but something looks different. What could it be? I know. I'll take a photo of the house with my digital camera every day. Then I can see if something has changed. I run upstairs and find my camera and then run back into the garden. My mum sees me.

"José, just forget about the house. We've got more important things to do today. You're starting your new school tomorrow."

"Oh, Mum. I'm trying to forget school." William comes into the garden and tries to lick my face. I almost fall over because he's so big. He's only about a year old and he's still getting bigger. I found him – or really he found me – after Christmas last year and he's stayed with us.

My new school

Monday morning! My favourite day – I don't think. I never liked it before. It's even worse now. When I started my new school last year, it was OK because everybody was new in

---

5 to find [faɪnd] suchen • 11 to lick [lɪk] ablecken • 13 to get [get] werden

Year 7, but now everybody in Year 8 will know each other and I won't know anyone.

"I'll go to school with you if you like," says my mum.

"Yes, and hold my hand and take me to the classroom," I say and then, more loudly, "Mum, I'm twelve! No, of course you can't take me to school." 5

"Well, have a good time and I'll see you when you come home."

• • •

I walk to school and try to find my tutor group. The school sent me a map and my tutor's name, but the school 10 is so big. I stand in the playground and look around me. Which way should I go? I should ask someone really, but everybody is talking to someone and nobody even looks at me. I want to go home, but I know I can't.

"Er, hello," I say to a girl. 15

"Hi," she says and walks on.

"Er, do you know where Mrs William's classroom is?" I ask two boys.

"Sorry, no, we're new here. We're in Year 7," they answer. Year 7? But they're so big. They're bigger than I am. Am I in 20 a school of giants?

"Excuse me. Can you tell me where Mrs William's classroom is?" I ask two teachers.

They look at me and start laughing. I just look at them. What have I said? What's so funny? 25

They take me to the classroom and I find out that they aren't teachers at all. They're in Year 12 and they needn't wear uniforms. They look so old. At my old school we didn't have a Year 12.

I finally find my tutor group. 30

"You must be José Jones," says Mrs Williams. "Are you Spanish?"

"Er, no. My dad was Spanish," I say.

2 not … anyone ['eniwʌn] niemand • 11 to stand in ['stænd‿ɪn] in/auf etwas stehen • 21 giant [dʒaɪənt] Riese • 26 to find out [faɪnd‿'aʊt] erfahren • 32 Spanish ['spænɪʃ] Spanisch

The teacher gives us our timetables, and then it's time to go to our first lessons.

"Phil, can you show José where your lessons are, please?"

5 Phil turns around and smiles. He looks nice. So maybe my day won't be so bad.

David

I come home from school and open the door with my key. William hears me, runs to the door and tries to run outside because he's so excited. Great! Someone (OK well:
10 something) is very happy to see me, but I can't get into the house because William is pushing against the door. Then the phone rings.

"William, let me in!" I shout and push the door open. At that moment William runs away from the door. The
15 door opens quickly, and I fall onto the floor. A second later William comes back with the phone.

"Hello," I say.

"Hello, it's me," says my friend, David, while William tries to wash my face. David is a friend from Manchester,
20 and it's really good to hear his voice.

"So how did it go?" he asks.

"Terrible," I answer. "Everybody thinks that I'm an idiot."

"Wow, they're quick in London. It took us a week before
25 we found out you were an idiot."

"Very funny."

"So what happened?" askes David.

"Well, this boy, Phil, showed me the school. And he's nice, but he's crazy about football. When I said that I come
30 from Manchester, he thought I must be a Manchester United fan. Then he and his friends wanted me to play football with them."

---

10 to get into [get ˈɪntə] hineinkommen • 11 to push [pʊʃ] drücken • 14 moment [ˈməʊmənt] Moment • 21 How did it go? [ˌhaʊ dɪd ɪt ˈgəʊ] Wie ist es gelaufen?

"Oh no, you didn't play with them, did you?"

"Well, what could I do?"

"But you can't play football!" said David.

"Yes, I know – and they knew that, too, after about five minutes, when someone kicked a ball and I caught it." 5

"But you can't do that! You use your feet in football. That's why it's called *football!*"

"Yes, I know, I know! But I didn't think. The ball came at me and I just opened my hands. And then, of course, someone shouted 'No way, José!' And everybody laughed 10 and so every time I did something silly, someone shouted –"

"No way, José!" finished David. "Not really original, is it? You hear it on TV all the time."

"Yeah, well, about five minutes later the ball hit me on 15 the nose, and I had to stop then."

"So was it any better after that?" he asks.

"No, it was worse. Everybody asked about my nose and when I told them, they laughed and said, 'No way, José!'"

"Can't you change your name? You always have 20 problems with it."

"Oh, I'd love to change it. We had our first Spanish lesson at school, and the teacher talked to me in Spanish for five minutes! When he finally stopped, I said that I don't speak Spanish. Of course, everybody laughed again. Well, 25 everybody except the teacher. He just looked angry."

"Oh, that's silly. But aren't there any nice kids there?"

"Yes. I told you. Phil is nice. But he's only interested in people for his football team. And there's this girl, Liz. She's really nice. But everybody likes her: She's the most 30 popular girl in school, I think. Today she asked me to sit next to her and her friends at lunchtime. And they were good fun, but …"

"But what? What did you do?"

---

5 to kick [kɪk] kicken • 5 to catch [kætʃ] fangen • 10 no way [nəʊ weɪ] das gibt's doch nicht! • 13 original [əˈrɪdʒnl] originell • 15 to hit [hɪt] treffen • 26 except [ɪkˈsept] außer • 29 Liz [lɪz] • 33 good fun [gʊd fʌn] *hier:* lustig

"I tried to tell a joke."

"No way, José."

"David!"

"Sorry. But I've told you before. Never tell jokes. You
always forget the end."

"Yes, well, of course nobody laughed. Then they talked
about my nose – it was still red – and they told me about
our History teacher She has a really big nose! Well, the
next lesson was History and I went in …"

"This doesn't sound good. What did you do, José?"

"Well, I looked at her nose and I thought, that's a big
nose. Then I heard the teacher say, 'José, can you hear
me?' and I answered, 'Yes, Miss Nose.'"

"Oh, José. You idiot. Nobody can help you!" said David –
when he finished laughing about five minutes later.

I tell David about the noises in the house next door.

"That's really exciting. They're probably ghosts," he
says.

"Oh, don't be silly, David."

"Well, maybe the old woman isn't really in hospital!"

"What?"

"Maybe her awful son has locked her in the house and
is stealing her money from her. Maybe he isn't feeding her!
Then she'll die quickly and he can have the house."

"People don't really do things like that."

"Some people do. Or maybe there are terrorists in there
and they have lots of weapons and …"

We talk more about the house next door, and then I
go into the garden and take another photo. I go to bed.
I feel scared and I can't sleep, but I don't hear any noises
tonight.

---

26 terrorist ['terəɪst] Terrorist • 27 weapon ['wepən] Waffe • 30 to feel scared
[fiːl 'skeəd] Angst haben

Sandra

The first week was bad, the second week was … better!
I told Phil that my uncle can get tickets for Manchester
United matches, and now he thinks that I'm wonderful
again. And I think that Liz is wonderful, but everybody
thinks she's wonderful. I can't talk to her much because ⁵
there are always lots of people around her. She must live
near me, though, because I see her sometimes when I walk
to school or home again. I always hope that I'll see her.

Now it's the third week. I'm thinking about her when
I leave the house with William on Monday evening. And ¹⁰
that's probably why I don't see the girl in front of our
house. William runs to the wall and I bump into the girl.
She shouts angrily and drops her bag. It's open and things
have fallen on the ground, so I help her to find them all
again. It's almost dark, so it's not so easy. She doesn't say ¹⁵
thank you. Her eyes are red. I say that I'm sorry, but she
doesn't look at me. She's looking in her bag for something,
so I just walk on with William.

I don't think about it again, but this morning when I
leave the house, I find a key on the ground. It must be the ²⁰
girl's. But how do I find her? I've never seen her before. I'm
late so I just put it in my pocket and go to school.

• • •

At lunchtime I'm eating my dinner at a table alone, and
I'm hoping that Liz will come and sit with me. Suddenly I
see her. She and her friends have got their dinner now and ²⁵
Liz looks up. When she sees me, she smiles. She's walking
towards me when I see another girl. Who's that? I know her
from somewhere, I'm sure. She sits down at a table in front
of mine and then I remember. She's the girl from yesterday
evening. While Liz and her friends are sitting down, I get ³⁰
up and give the girl her key back.

Sandra ['sændrə] • 7 though [ðəʊ] jedoch • 12 to bump into [bʌmp ˈɪntə] mit jmd
zusammenstoßen • 13 to drop [drɒp] etwas fallen lassen • 14 ground [graʊnd]
Boden • 22 pocket ['pɒkɪt] Tasche • 27 towards someone [təˈwɔːdz] auf jmd zu

"What are you doing with my key?" she shouts. "Why didn't you give it to me before? You're a thief and I'm going to get you after school!"

I don't say anything. I walk back to my table, but my legs
5 are shaking. Liz and her friends are looking at me. They're shocked, too. It's so embarrassing. Why does this have to happen in front of Liz?

"What was that about?" she asks me, and I tell them all about yesterday evening.

10 "You shouldn't go near her," Liz says, "She's trouble. She's in Year 10 and she often hits smaller kids. I don't know why the teachers let her stay at this school."

"Er, right," I say. Of course she just wanted to help, but I was scared before and I'm even more scared now.

15 When the bell rings, I leave school very quickly. I try to leave school before Sandra leaves her lesson, but she's already in the street outside school. She's with some

---

3 to get someone [gɛt] jemanden kriegen • 5 to shake [ʃeɪk] zittern • 6 shocked [ʃɒkt] schockiert • 6 embarrassing [ɪmˈbærəsɪŋ] peinlich • 6 to have to [ˈhəv tʊ] muss • 10 She's trouble [ʃiz ˈtrʌbl] *hier:* Sie macht nur Ärger

friends and they're waiting for me. I run and they run after me. They're older and bigger than me, but I'm fast and they stop after a few minutes.

• • •

It's Wednesday morning. I wake up and look at the clock. It's 8 o'clock, but I don't want to get up. I don't want to go to school. My mum calls me. 5

"Mum, I don't feel well. Can I stay at home?" I ask.

"What's the problem? Have you got a temperature?" she asks. She feels my head and looks in my mouth.

"I just don't feel well," I say. 10

William licks my face. He doesn't believe me either.

"Well, you don't look ill, and I've got something really important at work today. Go to school, and if you still feel ill, phone me up and I'll come," she says.

I go to school. I'm scared. I'm worried about Sandra. At 15 lunchtime I don't want to go to the playground, but I can't stay inside. I see Sandra and her friends. She points when she sees me and walks towards me. I look around and walk towards a teacher. She sees the teacher and stops. She smiles and waves at me. It isn't a nice smile. 20

• • •

Now it's half past three and I'm going home. I usually walk through the park, but I decide to go by bus today. When I get home, I run inside and close the door. I've made it. But I have to leave the house again. I need to take William for a walk. I take him to the park and he runs towards the 25 small lake. He wants to chase the ducks. As always! I shout to him, but he doesn't stop. He swims around in the lake behind the ducks. I think he's laughing at me. Everybody laughs at him – until he comes out. He runs to me and shakes himself. Everybody around him gets wet. The 30 children laugh, but a woman shouts.

7 I don't feel well [aɪ dəʊn ˈfiːl ˌwel] es geht mir nicht gut • 8 temperature [ˈtemprətʃə] Fieber • 9 to feel [fiːl] fühlen • 11 not … either [ˈaɪðə] auch nicht • 23 I've made it [ˌaɪv ˈmeɪd ˌɪt] Ich habe es geschafft. • 26 duck [dʌk] Ente • 29 to come out [kʌm ˈaʊt] herauskommen • 30 to shake himself [ˈʃeɪk ˌɪmself] sich schütteln

"Look at my skirt! I can't go into town like this …"

I leave with William quickly before she asks me to buy a new skirt.

• • •

On Thursday I don't see Sandra at all and I start to feel
5 better again. Maybe she's forgotten, I think. It's Friday now. Weekend! Great! I walk home through the park and listen to my MP3 player. I look around and can't see any people. I'm happier now. I'm almost at home when suddenly Sandra is standing in front of me. She's with her friends.
10 Where did she come from? She walks towards me. I want to run away, but my legs are shaking. Before I can move, she pushes me and I fall against a boy. The boy pushes me back again. Sandra hits me in my face, on my nose, and I fall to the ground. Then I hear other voices. I can't hear
15 what they're saying, but Sandra and her friends leave me.

I'm lying on the grass and holding my nose when Liz comes over to me. She was with her friends in the park when they saw Sandra. She saved me and I'm glad, but I feel terrible. I'm so embarrassed. Every day I've wanted to
20 meet Liz in the park, but not like this!

"Are you OK?" she asks.

"Yes, thanks," I say. "It was nothing really. Thanks a lot." I can't look at Liz's face.

Why must she see me like this?

25 "Can you walk home on your own?" she asks.

"Yes, thanks. I live just around the corner."

I still can't look at her. She must think I'm an idiot! She says goodbye and goes home.

Things that go bump in the night

When she sees me, my mum asks me what happened. I tell
30 her I walked into a tree. Things like that often happen, and so she believes me. David phones on Saturday, but I don't

---

12 to push [pʊʃ] schubsen • 16 to lie [laɪ] liegen • 19 I'm so embarrassed
[ɪmˈbærəst] es ist mir so peinlich • to go bump [bʌmp] rumsen, poltern

tell him about Sandra. I can't. I don't know why. I can't tell anybody. I have a terrible weekend, and on Monday I don't go to school. At night I can't sleep because I know I must go to school some day. I look at the clock. Four o'clock. Then I hear a noise next door. Then another noise, and I suddenly 5 have an idea. I'll go outside and look at the house. Maybe there's a light on. Or maybe I'll see somebody. William is sleeping. Should I take him with me? No. If there are thieves there, he'll only lick their faces. But I'll take my digital camera. 10

I go outside and into the garden. I leave the kitchen door open, and I watch the house next door. It's dark and I'm scared. I think I'll go in again, but then I see something white at the window. It looks like a face. I'm very scared. I take a photo with my camera. Suddenly I can't see 15 anything because it's so bright when the camera flashes. When I can see again, I run back towards our house, but just at that moment the door closes with a bang. It was the wind. I can't believe it. I'm in the garden in my pyjamas and I haven't got a key. I look at the house next door again. The 20 white face has gone. Did I really see it? Then I see it again. I bang on our door until my mum comes downstairs.

"What are you doing in the garden in your pyjamas?" she asks. "Have you gone bananas?"

She's angry. 25

"It's five o'clock in the morning." she says, "I thought you were ill."

"Mum, I heard a noise next door, so I went outside and then I saw something in the window," I tell her when she finally listens to me. 30

She stops and looks at me. She sits down.

"Are you sure?" she asks.

"Yes, I'm sure."

"Well, let's phone the police then."

• • •

2 not … anybody ['ɛnɪbɒdi] niemand • 4 some day ['sʌm deɪ] eines Tages •
16 to flash [flæʃ] blitzen • 19 pyjamas [pɪˈdʒɑːməz] Schlafanzug • 24 to go
bananas [ɡəʊ bəˈnɑːnəz] *hier:* verrückt werden

The police come. They look around the house, but all the doors and windows are closed. They go to the house and knock on the door. We run outside. William comes, too. He has just woken up.

5 "Why are you knocking?" I say to the policeman, "You'll scare them. They'll run away."

"Oh yes, what do you want us to do, young man? Break the door down?" says the policeman.

This policeman is not friendly. He thinks I'm an idiot.

10 "That only happens in films," he says, "We can't just break down people's doors."

Nobody opens the door. There are no noises in the house and no lights.

"But if they're stealing something, they won't open the
15 door when the police are there, will they?" I ask. I think that's a good point.

"Well, tell me this, young man. How do you think they got into the house? The doors and windows aren't broken."

"Er," I say, "Maybe they've got a key."

20 This sounds silly the moment I say it.

"Maybe you had a bad dream," says the policeman.

Then I have an idea. I take my digital camera out of my pocket. Maybe we can see something on one of the photos. I try to switch the camera on, but I can't. Typical! I
25 forgot to switch it off. The battery is empty.

"Did you hear the noises, too, Mrs Jones?"

"Er, no," she says, "but I believe my son. He's heard noises a few times and he says he saw something in the house."

30 I look at my mum. Does she really believe me? She's never said that before. Then I see that William is very interested in the policeman's leg. I want to pull him away before the policeman notices, but he asks me another question.

---

3 to knock [nɒk] klopfen • 7 to break … down [ˈbreɪk daʊn] aufbrechen •
9 friendly [ˈfrendli] freundlich • 22 to take out [ˈteɪk aʊt] herausnehmen • 24 to
switch on [swɪtʃ ˈɒn] einschalten • 25 to switch off [swɪtʃ ˈɒf] ausschalten • 32 to
pull [pʊl] ziehen • 33 to notice [ˈnəʊtɪs] bemerken

"Do you believe in ghosts?"

I don't answer him. It's a joke, I think. I don't believe in ghosts. Of course I don't. Just then I see William lift his leg.

"Come on, William. Let's go back to bed," I say and pull ⁵ him away back to the house.

"Thanks for coming anyway," says my mum.

When I look round, the policeman has just noticed that the leg of his trousers is all wet, and he's not happy.

Back to school

On Tuesday morning I charge the camera battery and ¹⁰ download the photos onto my computer. I'm excited. I'm sure I'll find something. Then everybody will believe me. But no, nothing. Just the house, again and again, and nothing in the window. The police are right: I'm an idiot.

In the afternoon my mum takes me to the doctor. ¹⁵ He can't find anything wrong with me.

"Have you had any problems at school?" he asks.

"No," I answer, maybe a little too quickly.

My mum looks at me now. Maybe she can see inside my head. On the way home she asks me about school, but I ²⁰ don't tell her about Sandra.

"You'll tell me if you have any problems, won't you?" she says. "You can always sort out problems when you talk about them."

That's what she thinks. Sandra will kill me if I tell ²⁵ someone. I know. And if they send her to another school, one of her friends will kill me.

I feel terrible when I wake up on Wednesday morning. I have to get up early and take William for a walk before school today. He's still sleeping when I'm ready to go. What ³⁰ a lazy dog! He just opens an eye when I wake him up, and

---

3 to lift [lɪft] heben • 10 to charge [tʃɑːdʒ] aufladen • 25 to kill [kɪl] umbringen • 31 lazy ['leɪzi] faul

he looks at me. I think he wants to ask me what I'm doing. He closes his eye again.

"Come on, William. We have to go. What kind of dog are you? Most dogs like walks. OK, we'll chase the ball," I say and find one in the corner.

Now he finally gets up and we go. I walk through the park quickly. Sandra won't be in the park at this time, will she? But I'm not sure. I see some girls behind me and try to walk faster, but William doesn't want to move. He's looking under a tree for the ball. Typical. The girls walk past. Sandra is not with them.

• • •

"Right! We're going for a run today," says our sports teacher.

Almost everybody complains, but I don't. Finally no football, no balls. I love running.

We run through a part of a forest near our school. It's great. I'm one of the fastest. Only Ryan is in front of me and Liz is just behind.

"OK. Let's have a race back to school." shouts the teacher, "Go, go, go!"

And I run and run. I'm only five metres behind Ryan now, but Liz is just behind me. I run faster. Just another hundred metres, but my stomach hurts. I can do it. I can do it. No, I can't. Liz can still run faster. She doesn't even look tired. I'm third.

"Great," says the teacher.

And I feel great, too. For the first time in a week!

"José, that was great. These two are the fastest runners in Year 8," he says and points at Ryan and Liz. They smile at me.

"Why don't you join their athletics club?" asks the teacher, "You're good enough. You could be a lot better."

"Yes, we're going after school," says Liz. "We've got

14 to complain [kəmˈpleɪn] sich beklagen • 17 one of the fastest [ˌwʌn̩ əv ðə ˈfɑːstɪst] einer der Schnellsten • 17 Ryan [raɪən] • 28 runner [ˈrʌnə] Läufer • 31 athletics [æθˈletɪks] Sport, Leichtathletik

orienteering today. Why don't you come, too?"

"Er, yes. I'd love to," I say, and I have no idea what orienteering is.

• • •

We walk together through the park. It's so nice. I'm not scared of Sandra now, but I feel a little embarrassed. This is the first time that I've spoken to Liz after she saved me from Sandra. She's very quiet. Is she thinking about that, too? I hope she doesn't want to talk about it. And then suddenly I see Sandra. Liz is watching her, too. Sandra is with some guys who are about 17 or 18, I think, but I haven't seen them at our school. We're walking towards them, and I see that they're throwing a mobile phone to each other. 5 10

"Hey, this is a great one," says one of the guys when he catches the mobile. "Smile!" he shouts, and then takes a photo of Sandra. 15

"Don't be an idiot," she says and looks very unhappy.

Liz and Ryan can see that, too.

---

1 orienteering [ɔːriən'tɪərɪŋ] Orientierungslauf • 10 guy [gaɪ] Typ

"I bet they've stolen that mobile!" shouts Ryan.

Sandra looks up and sees us. She's heard Ryan, I'm sure. She looks very angry, and I don't want to walk past them, but I don't have any choice.

5 "Why do you think that they've stolen it?" I ask quietly.

"They went to our school until last year, and then they had to leave because they stole things. I think they're called Frank and Steve," said Ryan.

"Yeah, they had big problems with the police," said Liz.

10 "Well, what should we do? Should we phone the police?" I ask.

"No, we can't. What could we say?" says Liz.

"Does Sandra steal things, too?" I ask, and I'm thinking about the house next door. Maybe she goes in and steals 15 things, and this is the reason for the noises.

"I don't think so," says Ryan, "She just hits people." Liz is very quiet.

Sandra turns and looks at me, and I look the other way.

Orienteering

"This is José," says Liz.

20 "Hi. Have you ever been orienteering?" asks Geoff, the trainer.

"Er, no," I say.

"And do you know what orienteering is?" he asks.

"Er, no," I answer again and I feel embarrassed.

25 Liz and Ryan look at me and laugh.

"Will you two take him with you?" asks Geoff and looks at Liz and Ryan.

"And don't lose him!" he laughs. "We'll talk when you come back."

30 Lose me? Where are we going? What are we going to do?

• • •

1 to bet [bet] wetten, dass • 4 not … a choice [tʃɔɪs] keine Wahl • 20 Geoff [dʒef]

Half an hour later we're all in the middle of the forest, and we're trying to decide where to go.

"We should go this way," says Ryan.

"No, look," says Liz. "Look, I think we're here on the map. There are those trees there, and we're at the top of the hill." 5

"Oh yes," says Ryan. "You're right. We must be here, so we should go that way. Down that path."

I'm still looking at the map. How do they know that? Then I run after them as fast as I can. But I can't run fast now because my legs are so tired. The grass is wet and I fall over and slide down the hill. First Ryan and Liz just laugh and let me slide past them, but then they think it looks like fun. They both jump down onto the grass and slide after me, too. Then we land on top of each other and laugh and laugh. 10 15

3 to go this way [gəʊ 'ðɪs weɪ] hier entlang gehen • 12 to slide down ['slaɪ daʊn] herunter rutschen • 14 to jump down onto the grass ['dʒʌmp daʊn ˌɒntuː] ins Gras springen

"Did you enjoy it?" asks Geoff an hour later when we are back at the athletics club.

We've had to run through the forest from control point to control point as quickly as we could. Geoff drew the
5 control points on the map so we (well, Liz and Ryan) could read the map and then run to them.

"Yes, it was great," I answer, although I'm really tired. "But I have no idea how to read a map."

"You'll learn," he answers. "Can you two show him some
10 of the symbols? And I'll give you a map for next week and some notes about it. Here you are. Oh, but do you want to come next week?"

"Oh, yes please!"

"Well, we've got training again on Friday. At seven
15 o'clock. We're just going to run this time."

• • •

We go and have a shower. When I've finished, I see that it's almost six o'clock. I'm late. My mum will be worried so I switch my mobile on. Someone's sent me a text. Great. Probably David. I want to tell him about orienteering now.
20 It was so good. I look at the message: U R dead.

My heart stops. Who sent that? It must be Sandra. Where did she find my number? What can I do now? I sit down.

"Are you OK?" asks Ryan. "You look green."

"Oh no. You've found out my secret," I say, and find out
25 that I can still laugh a little. "I'm an alien and the shower has just washed the paint away."

"Oh we knew that," laughs Ryan. "You come from Manchester!"

Liz laughs, too, and then asks, "Are you OK?"

30 "I just feel a bit sick," I say and turn the mobile off again.

"Yeah, I know. We ran a lot today, didn't we? I know what we need …"

---

3 control point [kən'trəʊl pɔɪnt] Orientierungspunkt • 10 symbol ['sɪmbl] Symbol
• 16 to have a shower [həv‿ə 'ʃaʊə] *hier:* sich duschen • 30 to feel a bit sick
['fiːl‿ə bɪt ˌsɪk] sich ein bisschen schlecht fühlen

"Some chocolate," says Ryan, and I know that isn't the first time he's said it. "Liz loves chocolate. If you ever want to make her happy, just buy her some chocolate," he says to me. I look at her and she's smiling at me. I almost forget the message. Almost – but not quite. 5

We buy some chocolate at a shop and then we walk home with Liz because it's getting dark now. She lives near the park and Ryan lives near me, so we walk on together for some time.

"So when did you start orienteering?" I ask him. 10

"Last year. One of my friends did it, so I went, too. He lives in another part of London now, so he's stopped orienteering. But I love it. Sometimes we go at night. That's even more fun. We have a great laugh and someone always falls in some water." 15

We talk some more and then I run the last 200 metres to my house. I walk through the door and feel safe at last. A mistake! I forgot my mother.

"Where have you been?" she shouts.

I don't even try to answer. I know that she's going to 20 shout for another five minutes.

"I've been really worried about you. I wanted to phone the police. Why didn't you phone me? You have a mobile, don't you? And why didn't you switch it on? I couldn't even phone you … And yes, I took William for a walk. I thought 25 I would find you in the park under a tree."

I remember the message now and can't think of anything else.

• • •

That night I can't sleep. I don't know what to do about Sandra. I can't live like this. Then I think I hear her voice. 30

"No, you must take those away from here. He knows. I'm sure he knows," the voice says. Is that Sandra?

---

5 not quite [nɒt 'kwaɪt] nicht ganz • 14 to have a great laugh [ˌhəv ə greɪt 'lɑːf] *hier:* viel Spaß haben • 26 would [wəd] würde • 27 not … anything else [els] nichts anderes

Am I dreaming? Am I crazy? Then I hear another noise next door. Oh no. Not that as well. I find my MP3 player and listen to some music. William comes and lies on my bed. Sometimes I think he knows how I feel.

Friends

5 I listen to music all night and feel ill the next morning. Mum can see it. I stay in bed until lunchtime, but I still can't sleep.

"Do you want something to eat?" asks my mum when I get up.

10 "No thanks. I'm not hungry."

"Are you worried about something? You know, you've missed three days at school now and that's not good."

"No, I know," I answer and look at the floor.

I'm sleeping in front of the TV when suddenly a loud
15 bang wakes me up. I jump up. Did the noise come from next door? Then I hear my mum. Oh, it's just somebody at the door. I close my eyes again – it can't be for me.

"José, some of your friends are here. Do you want to see them?"

20 My friends? I open my eyes again and panic. Has Sandra found out where I live? What should I do? My mum looks worried.

"They're called Ryan and Liz. They just want to know if you're OK. They said you looked very green yesterday. I can
25 tell them you're too ill and you don't want to see them," she says when I still don't answer.

"No, no, I'd like to see them. I feel better now."

As the door opens, William runs in from the kitchen. He jumps up and tries to lick Liz's face. I try to pull him away,
30 but I'm too late. Liz lands on the floor.

---

3 to lie [laɪ] sich hinlegen • 4 how I feel [haʊˌaɪ ˈfiːl] wie es mir geht • 15 to wake … up [ˈweɪk … ˌʌp] jemanden aufwecken

24

Oh no, that was the end of a beautiful friendship, I think, but when I pull William away, I see that Liz is laughing.

"We've brought you something," says Liz when she stands up.

"Chocolate?" I ask.   5

"Homework," says Ryan.

"Mum, I'm too ill to see them. They want to leave now," I shout.

Liz and Ryan laugh.

"We've got a test next week in Mr Scott's class, and he   10
asked us to give you your homework."

"Oh, I don't feel good. I think I'm going to be ill for another two weeks," I joke.

"No, you can't," says Liz. "We've only got another week and a half at school, and then we've got holiday for a   15
week."

"Oh, OK. Well, just a week and a half then."

"I must go now," says Ryan after a few more minutes, "but I always walk past your house on the way to school. Should I call tomorrow morning? Or will you still be too   20
ill?"

---

1 friendship ['frenʃɪp] Freundschaft • 10 test [test] Test, Klausur • 13 to joke [dʒəʊk] scherzen • 20 to call [kɔːl] vorbeikommen

Bullies

On Friday I walk to school with Ryan. I feel safer, but I still look around for Sandra. I see her at school, but she doesn't come near me when Ryan or Liz are there. I meet Ryan and Liz after school and we all go back to my house. We want to
5 eat something before we go to the athletics club. It's great when Liz and Ryan are there with me, but they can't be there all the time. I must do something. But what? I look at Liz. She's watching me. Can she see what I'm thinking?

"Are you still having problems with Sandra?" she asks.
10 "Er, no," I say and look down again.

"José, I know how you feel. I know what it's like when somebody bullies you," she says.

"You! How can *you* know?" I say angrily, because I don't believe her, and I don't want to talk about it.
15 "Some girls bullied me last year," she says.

"You?" I repeat. I still can't believe it.

"Yes. Some girls from school always walked past my house and … ."

"You haven't seen Liz's house," said Ryan, "It's nice. Very
20 nice."

And I know they've talked about this before.

"Yes, it is. My parents have got lots of money. I know, I'm lucky. And anyway, one day I dropped my bag and these girls were behind me. They picked it up and looked
25 in, and then they said, 'Do you want your bag back? Well, give us some money now.' I gave them some money. I was so scared, I didn't know what to do. After that they often wanted money from me, and I gave it to them. I was scared all the time. I never wanted to leave the house. I didn't tell
30 my parents or the teachers or my friends, and I became ill."

Liz is talking very quickly and quietly. She's almost crying. I can see that it still hurts her even now.

---

bully ['bʊli] jemand, der andere Schüler tyrannisiert oder mobbt • 15 to bully ['bʊli] tyrannisieren, mobben • 30 became [bɪ'keɪm] wurde

"What did you do?" I ask quietly.

"Well, one day an older girl saw what happened and she came and helped me. She walked to school with me and we talked to a teacher, and he helped me too. The girl knew the other girls' names and told the teacher. The teacher told the police, and the police went to see the girls and their parents. It was awful. I was so scared. I thought they would kill me. But anyway, that was the end of my problems. The police were really good, and the teachers at school were really nice, too. It's very difficult, but you must tell somebody. People can help you."

"And what about the girls? Do they still go to our school?"

"One of them still does," she said and was quiet for a second. "It's Sandra. When she sees me, she looks the other way. I don't know what the police said to her, but I think she's scared of me now. I didn't want to tell you, José, because I didn't want to scare you."

I almost fall over.

Now I tell them about Sandra and how she has bullied me. They say they'll come with me on Monday and see a teacher with me. It was easier than I thought, and I feel better already.

We go running again, and I run and run and I think that I can do anything now.

"Let's meet tomorrow," says Liz when we leave the club. "We can practise orienteering again."

• • •

I feel really happy when I arrive home. When David phones in the evening, I tell him all about orienteering and about my new friends, and we laugh a lot. Then he asks me about the noises in the house next door. I tell him about how William wet the policeman's leg.

When I go to bed, I think about Liz and Ryan and orienteering, and how lucky I am to have some new friends.

---

32 to wet [wet] *hier:* anpinkeln

Then I think about Sandra. Why does she bully me? What have I done? We haven't got a nice house and she doesn't want lots of money from me. So why does she hit me? How did it start? Oh, yes. When I gave her that key back. So why
5 was she angry? I don't understand it.

That key! Was there something special about it?

A photo

The next day we go orienteering in the forest, and then we come back to my house again. Outside my house, I stop and look at the house next door again. Now something
10 looks different!

"Does nobody live there?" asks Ryan when he sees that I'm looking at the house. "The curtains are never open."

I tell them all about the noises, and they think it's really exciting.

15 "Have you never tried to look in the house?" asks Liz when we're sitting in the living room.

I tell them about how I went into the garden in the middle of the night and saw a face at the window. I also tell them how I was so scared that I ran back to the house,
20 but the door closed before I could go in.

"Didn't you call the police?" asks Ryan when he stops laughing.

"Yes, we did and they came, but they didn't find anything. I don't think that they believed me."

25 "Why didn't you take a photo?" asks Liz.

"I did! I've taken lots of pictures!" I say.

"And what was on them?" asks Liz.

"Nothing," I say.

"Nothing?" asks Liz. "Are you sure?"

30 "Well, I couldn't see anything. Just lots of pictures of the house."

---

26 I did! [aɪ ˈdɪd] *hier:* Hab' ich doch!

"Let's all look at them together now," says Liz. "Maybe we'll find something. Just a little thing. Something that's changed. Maybe a curtain is in a different place, or a window is open or something."

We run upstairs and I switch the computer on. Oh, it's so slow. Why is it so slow? While we're waiting for the computer, we talk about the house next door.

"Oh, I've just had an idea," I say.

"No way, José! Quick, write that down – *Saturday, October 10th: José had an idea,*" laughs Ryan.

"Very funny. You know what! I think maybe Sandra has something to do with the noises in the house," I say.

"Why?" ask Liz and Ryan together.

"Well, when I bumped into her and her bag fell on the ground, she was outside the house next door. Why was she here? And what about the key from her bag? Maybe it's the key to the door. And …"

"Oh yes," says Ryan, and he's excited now. "Maybe it's the key to the house, and maybe that's the reason she's so awful to you! She thinks that you know about her."

"But why should she go in the house?" says Liz.

"Maybe she steals things from it."

"But when you steal things from a house, you don't go back again and again, do you?" asks Liz. "And why does she have the key then?"

We can't answer the questions, and we talk about other ideas for some time. Finally the computer's ready. Ryan and Liz are very excited. I'm not. I know there's nothing on the photos.

"Oh come on. They're too dark," says Ryan. "Didn't you try to make them lighter?"

"Er, no," I say. "How do you do that?"

"No way, José. Don't you know anything?"

"Well, I've only had my digital camera a few …" I start, but Ryan and Liz aren't listening. They're working on the

31 lighter ['laɪtə] heller

photos. They're making all the photos lighter and easier to see.

After about another ten minutes Liz suddenly shouts, "Look! Look! There's a face!"

5 We look. It is a face. There's a man or boy behind a tree near the house. Someone was in the garden while I was outside on that night last week. Even the idea is scary.

"I know that face," says Liz, "I've seen him before. But where?"

10 "I know," says Ryan. "We saw him and another guy with Sandra in the park last week. I think this guy's name is Frank."

We look at each other. We're all thinking the same thing.

15 "They steal mobile phones and hide them in the house," says Liz slowly.

"Yes, it's perfect. Sandra has a key, and they can go in and out of the house when they want," I say. "And one night I thought I heard Sandra's voice outside. She said
20 something like, 'You must take those away.' Maybe she meant the phones."

"But why should she say that? She wants to hide the phones there, doesn't she?" asks Ryan.

"I don't know, maybe she doesn't. She didn't look happy
25 when she was with those guys last week."

"Oh, we must do something," says Liz. "Should we phone the police?"

"But what can we say? We still can't *prove* anything," I say.

30 "I know. Let's watch the house," says Liz. "We can see what's happening, and then we can phone the police. What time do you usually hear noises?"

"Well, sometimes I hear noises quite early. About nine o'clock maybe – and sometimes a lot later."

33 quite [kwaɪt] ziemlich

William finds a clue

That night Liz and Ryan and William and I are all sitting in the back garden of the house next door. We're sitting in the back garden because we can't hide in the street. I've got three pullovers and a big winter jacket on, and I'm still cold. 5

"Should we go home now and have a warm drink?" I ask. "I'm cold and they probably won't come at all."

"José, we've only been here ten minutes."

We wait ten minutes longer. It's not exciting at all now. We can't talk too much because someone could hear us. 10

"You know, I think we should go home now and have a warm drink," says Ryan ten minutes later.

"Ryan, what kind of wimp are you?" I ask and everybody laughs.

• • •

At about 11 o'clock we hear a noise, and then we see a 15 light in the cellar of the house. Ryan goes nearer to the house very quietly and looks through the window. Then he waves. We go and look and see Sandra's friends with big boxes in their hands. It's very scary. What if they see us?

"What are they doing?" says Liz very quietly. "They're 20 carrying the boxes out of the house, not into the house."

"Maybe there are a lot of mobile phones in there. Maybe they're moving them because they want to sell them," I say.

"Or maybe they're moving them because they want to 25 hide them in another place. Maybe they think you know what's happening," says Liz to me. "What should we do now?"

"Let's phone the police," says Ryan, but then one of the guys switches the light off. 30

"They must have the last boxes. Listen! They're putting them into a car. Let's go and stop them," says Liz.

13 wimp [wɪmp] Weichei, Feigling • 16 cellar [ˈselə] Keller • 21 out [aʊt] aus

We don't ask how we're going to stop them. We just run into the street.

They're getting into the car, and Frank seems to push Sandra into the car. Doesn't she want to go?

5 "Stop," shouts Ryan, but the engine is running and nobody hears him. William runs at the car and at one of the guys. He's got something in his hand, something that must look interesting to William.

"Come back, William!" I shout. I don't want them to hurt 10 him, but just then one of the guys kicks him, and he falls to the ground. I run to William and they all drive away in the car.

---

3 to get into [get ˈɪntə] einsteigen • 5 engine [ˈendʒɪn] Motor

"Oh no. What are we going to do now?"

"I'm going to phone the police," says Ryan and he takes out his mobile.

William is making some funny noises. The man hurt him, I think. He's got some paper in his mouth. 5

"William has got a part of a map," I shout, surprised.

Ryan and Liz come quickly and look.

"It's part of the forest near here," says Liz. "Look, there's that little river and there's the old hut."

"A hut?" I say. "Do you think they're taking those boxes 10 there?"

"Let's go and look," says Liz.

"But there are two huts. Look here," says Ryan as he shows us the map. "Which one should we go to?"

"I know, I'll go to that one with William, and you two go 15 to the other one," I say. The huts are near to each other, so when anyone sees Sandra and her friends, they can phone the police and then phone the others."

"But José, you've never done orienteering at night," says Liz. "It's not so easy. Why don't you come with me, and 20 Ryan can go with William?"

"William won't want to go with Ryan, and we'll be together until we're near the huts," I say. I hope that they don't hear that my knees are banging together because I'm so scared. 25

OK José

Now I'm in the forest alone with William. I've just left Ryan and Liz, and the forest seems very dark. They've shown me the way to the hut and it's not far now, maybe half a mile or so. When I find it, it looks like nobody has been there for a long time. They must be at the other hut – or maybe 30 we're wrong altogether. Maybe Sandra and her friends are

---

5 paper ['peɪpə] Papier • 9 hut [hʌt] Hütte • 24 to bang together [ˌbæŋ təˈɡeðə] zittern, schlottern • 28 far [fɑː] weit weg • 31 to be wrong altogether [ˌrɒŋ ɔːltəˈɡeðə] vollkommen falsch liegen

going home, and they had a map with them because they like orienteering.

Well OK – maybe not.

I go towards the other hut. Ryan and Liz must be there
5 by now. Why haven't they phoned me? The other hut is easy to find. I just walk along a path and then turn left into another path. I can see the other hut now. It looks old too, but there's a light on in this one! William and I walk very quietly towards the hut and look in through the window,
10 but then I run away again quickly. Sandra and her friends are in the hut, and Ryan and Liz are in there, too. Ryan and Liz are on the sofa and they're tied up. I phone the police and tell them what's happening. The police say that I shouldn't do anything. I should just sit and wait. Well,
15 I don't want to do anything. What can I do against three older teenagers?

But then I want to know what is happening. I walk back to the hut and look in the window again, and I see that Steve has got a knife. Oh no! He's going to kill them. I must
20 do something. What can I do? Then I have an idea. I tell William what he must do, and then I find a stone and throw it through the window. The window breaks and William runs after the stone. I run towards the door because I want to break it down, but it's open. I fall on the floor. It's chaos,
25 but I hear Ryan shout, "OK José!" Steve turns to William, but William bites his arm and the knife falls on the floor. Then Sandra pushes Frank and he falls over a box. Sandra? Why does she push him? I take the knife and cut Liz and Ryan free. Just then the police arrive.
30 I can't believe it all now. It's like a dream or a TV programme. The police catch the guys and take them to the police cars. Sandra cries and cries and I hear her say, "It wasn't me. I didn't want to help them. They stole things.

---

6 along [əˈlɒŋ] entlang • 12 tied up [taɪd ˈʌp] festgebunden, gefesselt •
16 teenager [ˈtiːneɪdʒə] Teenager • 21 stone [stəʊn] Stein • 25 chaos [ˈkeɪɒs]
Chaos • 31 to catch [kætʃ] fassen, festnehmen

I didn't. I took them to my grandmother's house because they wanted a place to hide these things. I didn't want to take them there, but they scared me. I never stole anything! Oh, please believe me. My dad will kill me."

"Oh, the poor girl," says Liz.   5

"Yes, I thinks she's more scared than I was," I say.

A policewoman has just looked in all the boxes and now she's coming to us.

"Well done," she says. "These boys have stolen a lot of things from the shops and from people in the area. You 10
caught them, and a lot of people will be happy about it. You were very brave, you three. But that was very dangerous, and we told you to wait."

"But José saved us. I was really scared in there," Liz says.   15

"I wanted to wait for the police," I say, "but when I saw the knife and I knew he wanted to kill you, …"

"A knife? They wanted to kill you?" asks the policewoman.

"Well, er, no. Er, he just wanted to, er, open the box on 20
the floor," says Liz.

I look at her and Liz and Ryan look at me. We all know the mistake I made now and then they laugh and I laugh. We're still laughing five minutes later when the police want to take us home.   25

"But you were brilliant, José," says Liz in the police car. She moves towards me. Is she going to kiss me? I close my eyes and I suddenly feel a cold, wet tongue all over my face. It's William.

"Yes, William. You were brilliant, too," says Liz and gives 30
him a kiss.

---

5 poor [pɔː] arm • 11 caught [kɔːt] fasste, nahm fest • 31 kiss [kɪs] Kuss

Exercises

New house, new school

1. *Fill in the word grid to find out the answer to question 7 below. The page numbers will help you.*

1. The house next to José's is … . (page 5)
2. José has moved to London because José's mum has got a new … . (page 5)
3. Phil is in José's class and he's crazy about … . (page 8)
4. José's favourite person at school is … . (page 9)
5. David is José's old friend from … . (page 8)
6. José hears … in the house next door. (page 5)
7. Who does José have problems with later? The _____

2. *Describe in your own words what happens on José's first day at school.*

3. *What happened on your first day at the school you are at now? How did you feel? Compare your first day with a partner's first day.*

Sandra

José meets Sandra in the third week of school.
Find four sentences in the word snake below and write
them under "What happened". Then complete José's table.

snakehitmelbumpedintosandrasandrasmiledatmelgavesandraherkey

	Where	When	What happened
Monday			
Tuesday			
Wednesday			
Thursday			
Friday			

Things that go bump in the night

With some friends do a role play about what happens
between José, the policeman and Mrs Jones in this part of
the story.
Or: Write the police report.

Back to school

1. *Why does José feel excited, terrible, great, embarrassed?*

2. *On page 20, line 14 it says, "Maybe she goes in and*
   steals things, and this is the reason for the noises."
   Why does José think Sandra goes in and steals things?

Friends and bullies

Complete the crossword.

DOWN: (1) What does José hope Ryan and Liz have brought him? (3) How does José feel when he walks to school with Ryan on Friday?

ACROSS: (1) José hears Sandra's voice at night and thinks he's … (4) Who bullied Liz? (2) What did they want from Liz? (5) How does José feel when he has spoken to Liz and Ryan?

The end of the story

1. *Later the policewoman does interviews with everybody and writes notes about what happened.*
   Can you help her put the notes in the right order?

   a) Frank and Steve hide mobile phones that they have stolen in the house.
   b) Sandra takes Frank and Steve to her grandma's house.
   c) José and friends follow Frank, Steve and Sandra.
   d) Frank and Steve carry boxes to car and then leave.
   e) José and friends hide in the garden and watch the house.
   f) José sees Liz and Ryan in the hut - they're tied up.

2. *Who said these things during the interviews with the policewoman?*

a) "We didn't steal the mobiles. We found them in the forest."
b) "I took a photo one night and saw on it that Frank was in the garden next door. So we decided to watch the house."
c) "William, José's dog, took a map from Steve and I saw that the map showed the huts in the forest near José's house."

After reading

1. *Look at what you wrote down for question 3, "Before you read the story". Did you guess right? How was the story different? How was it the same?*

2. *Has someone ever bullied you or a friend? What did you/your friend do? What more can you do?*

Solutions

Before you read the story *(Musterlösung)*

1. Three children are falling/jumping down a hill. They look happy.
2. I think it means José saves something or somebody.
3. The story must be about noises in a house. Maybe somebody steals some mobiles and José finds them. The thieves try and kill him.

New house, new school

1. 1. empty; 2. job; 3. football; 4. Liz; 5. Manchester; 6. noises; 7. police

2. Everything went wrong. He couldn't find his classroom. All the pupils thought he was silly, and he had problems with two teachers.
3. –

Sandra

Monday: outside the house/in the evening/I bumped into Sandra.
Tuesday: at school/at lunchtime/I gave Sandra her key.
Wednesday: in the playground/at lunchtime/Sandra smiled at me.
Friday: in the park/after school/she hit me

Things that go bump in the night

Musterlösung: Police report: A boy heard noises in the house next door to his house and called us. He called us because the house was empty. We looked at the house, but the doors and windows were locked and there was nobody in there.

Back to school

1. José feels excited at home because he thinks he'll see something on the photos on his digital camera. He feels terrible when he wakes up because he has to go back to school. He feels great after the sports lesson because he loves running. He feels embarrassed because he hasn't talked to Liz since she rescued him from Sandra.
2. He knows that the guys she's with have stolen things.

Friends and bullies

Down: 1. chocolate; 3. safer
Across: 1. crazy, 4. girls; 2. money; 5. better

The end of the story

1. b, a, e, d, c, f
2. a. Steve or Frank; b. José; c. Liz

After reading

1. –
2. You can talk to teachers, parents or the police. Or phone a help line.